The One You Feed

Helping Churches Develop Spirit Fed Worship

Dan McGowan

ISBN: 9781520859248
ISBN-13: 9781520859248

DEDICATION

As is this case with every book I've written on the topic of worship (this makes the third), I dedicate this book to all who serve in the constantly-changing, usually exhilarating and almost always unstable ministry of music and worship leadership.

May God continue to work in you, and through you, as you strive to accomplish what He has gifted and called you to accomplish – namely, the impossible.

DISCLAIMER

I feel the need to open this book with a disclaimer that might surprise you:

There is no such thing as a "worship style"

Yes, you read that correctly. Countless books, articles, blogs and more on so called "worship styles" have been written about at length and, to be honest, they never "solve" the problem.

You know why? Because modern believers have mistakenly defined "worship styles" by "music styles" – which is a completely unfair and inaccurate way to define authentic worship.

The reason for my disclaimer is that most who will pick up this book will flip through the pages assuming it is another book on the evils of contemporary worship. They will think I am speaking against a "style of worship." But please hear me - this book is not about worship styles at all!

No, really, it's not!

I encourage you to read the introduction fully and, if after doing so, you still believe this book is dismantling worship styles then I have not done my job as a writer – or – perhaps you have opened these pages with a pre-conceived assumption that is not accurate nor fair to the writing.

I am fully confident that if you give this book a fair reading and try as much as possible to set your personal "worship agendas" aside you just might expand your knowledge and thinking on the important topic of "worship."

Blessings,

Dan McGowan

Dan McGowan

CONTENTS

PREFACE

As my passion for leading worship in various Christian circles grew, I found myself drawn to a wide selection of books debating everything from song style to demonic-influenced music and more. As I read these books I always walked away feeling agitated, angry and annoyed. Deep in my heart I never felt like any of these books truly got to the nugget of the issue. It is possible, of course, that I may not have read the correct books. My hope is to write a book that brings to light areas of worship and worship leading that need to be altered so that we can encounter the presence of God in our services and help others do the same.

Most reading this book completely understand, and have lived through, the angst of so-called "worship wars." Battle lines were drawn. (Perhaps they still are for some.) This saddens me. It is so unfortunate that the one area where God's people should be united in their glory of the Creator of everything we have ever, or will ever know, would end up scuffling over things like tempos, instruments, song style, pitchy vocals, droning organs, robes, drums, and more.

I honestly believe I have landed on a key to help unlock the mystery of our continual issues with worship in the church. And believe it or not, it has nothing to do with styles.

So – read on and let's see where the path leads us...

INTRODUCTION

I have been involved in some level of professional ministry for about 40 years including youth leader, Sunday school teacher, elder, creative media developer and music and worship ministry director.

Over the years, there has been one question that continues to poke at me begging for an answer: With all the resources we have at our avail, why is it that most churches across the country are simply ineffective at what they do?

I realize that sounds like a broad criticism. Perhaps it is. But the fact remains that most of you who will read this book are part of a church that either you or others wish could do a better job of being effective and impacting as a church. Nobody knows exactly how to define that, of course, but the majority of us want our churches to be "better."

Let me also state for the record that there are many churches who do seem to be doing things in a way that is consistently effective and impacting. This book is not really aimed at those churches. If your church has all the pistons popping at the right time, and in the right way, and you see lives being transformed by the Holy Spirit in your congregations then praise God! Put this book down and go buy a different book that will help you with your particular issues.

But perhaps you do attend a church that needs to rethink and reshape what you do in order to be "the church" as she is designed to be.

As you will soon discover, I happen to believe that the solution to the church's lack of truly impacting the world around us on a grand scale has to do with "food choices." (Don't worry, that will makes sense soon.)

This book is primarily focusing on the worship practices in today's churches. I fully realize that, often times, a book about "worship problems" ends up being a criticism of how contemporary worship has ruined churches by ignoring traditional worship. And that is sad. What's ever sadder is that criticism over new vs. old ways to worship almost always ends up as (or begins as) a discussion of "worship styles."

I want to do my best to assure you that this book is NOT a criticism of "modern" or "contemporary" worship. That said, there is a reason this sort of criticism comes so easily today: because we Christian have been trained to view worship *externally* rather than *internally*, which is what had led to our wrong use of the term "worship styles."

I recall a time when I saw a church member at a mid-week meeting whom I had not seen at church in recent weeks. I asked him where he had been. This is what he said:

"I go to (name of other church) to get my worship!"

Innocent enough on the surface. Until you realize that this was a comment made to me by a young elder in that church. His underlying premise was that, because our church offered what is today called "a blended worship format," he was unable to worship in the church where he served as an elder. He wanted something hipper. He wanted something edgier. He wanted the lights, the fog machine, the energetic band…

He wanted the show.

And he wanted these things because he had been wrongly trained to expect them.

He didn't know it at the time, but his comment is actually one of the things that motivated me to write this book.

A book on the topic of "worship" is always dangerous. (I believe some of the reasons for that will become evident as you read the following pages.) Every pastor, worship leader, musician, elder, deacon, even pew-sitter seems to be settled on what worship means – *for them*. At some point in their faith journey they arrived at a worship mindset that "works" for them or with which they are comfortable. Or, they look around at other churches and decide (as one might decide the grass is greener in their neighbor's yard) that the church down the street has more of what they want out of worship.

"…more of what they want out of worship…"

On the outset, that sentence doesn't really sound all that bad, does it? If we are honest, most of us who attend church do desire to "get something out of it." That comment even pops up in our dialogue from time to time when discussing worship. We speak of worship as if it is intended to give us something.

But, is the purpose of worship to give us something? Is "worship" a commodity? Don't answer too hastily because your answer may not be as noble as you assume.

I want to lovingly warn we Christians that today's churches are treading on dangerous ground. I fear we are creating what I call "faux worship." The word "faux" is defined as: "artificial, imitation, fake" and it seems like the best word to describe what I am hoping to convey.

The premise of this book is that, in general terms, there are two types of worship we can pursue: worship that **feeds the flesh** or worship that **feeds the Spirit**. The danger is that the illusion of worship laced in a flesh-fed environment can be deceiving and, thus, become, at best, "faux worship," and at worst, an idol.

I'm using the following scripture as a bold jumping off point...

Galatians 5:13-26

13 You, my brothers and sisters, were called to be free. But do not use your freedom to indulge the flesh; rather, serve one another humbly in love. 14 For the entire law is fulfilled in keeping this one command: "Love your neighbor as yourself." 15 If you bite and devour each other, watch out or you will be destroyed by each other.

16 So I say, walk by the Spirit, and you will not gratify the desires of the flesh. 17 For the flesh desires what is contrary to the Spirit, and the Spirit what is contrary to the flesh. They are in conflict with each other, so that you are not to do whatever you want. 18 But if you are led by the Spirit, you are not under the law.

19 The acts of the flesh are obvious: sexual immorality, impurity and debauchery; 20 idolatry and witchcraft; hatred, discord, jealousy, fits of rage, selfish ambition, dissensions, factions 21 and envy; drunkenness, orgies, and the like. I warn you, as I did before, that those who live like this will not inherit the kingdom of God.

22 But the fruit of the Spirit is love, joy, peace, patience, kindness, goodness, faithfulness, 23 gentleness and self-control. Against such things there is no law. 24 Those who belong to Christ Jesus have crucified the flesh with its passions and desires. 25 Since we live by the Spirit, let us keep in step with the Spirit. 26 Let us not become conceited, provoking and envying each other.

Just curious – did you do as I often do and simply skip past that passage of scripture to save time? You thought, "Oh, I know this passage…" I encourage you to stop right now, go back, and read it through as if you are reading it for the first time.

You didn't go back and do that, did you? I'll wait…

In that passage it's fairly easy to pin-point where being focused on the Holy Spirit can lead: Love, Joy, Peace, Patience, Kindness, Goodness, Faithfulness, Gentleness and Self-Control.

The next part, dealing with acts of the flesh, needs some unpacking. I have actually split the acts of flesh into two groups.

Group A includes the obvious sin-issue that are (hopefully) not present in a church. These include: sexual immorality, impurity, debauchery, witchcraft, drunkenness, orgies – and similar issues.

Group B is less obvious, more subtle and, sadly, often seen in churches: idolatry, hatred, discord, jealousy, fits of rage, selfish ambition, dissensions, factions and envy.

Keep in mind that both groups are linked together for a reason: because all the issues mentioned are destructive and, as verse 17 states, "contrary to the Spirit."

I want to assure you, again that this book **will not be a criticism on any particular style of worship** but, rather, a criticism of how we have somewhat accidently re-worked or re-defined and actually altered worship over the years.

WHY AM I WRITING THIS BOOK?

I never thought I'd use the phrase "a labor of love" in my life. I always found that phrase a bit cliché to be honest. But, this book truly has been a labor of love for me. There have been moments of joy, delight, anger, frustration and sadness all along the way. This is because I believe the topic is, perhaps, one of the most important topics we Christians (especially those of us who plan and program worship gatherings) need to examine. So, why am I writing this book?

I've asked myself that question several times on this journey!

I have wondered if we actually need another book on the topic of worship. My answer, of course, and quite obviously, is "yes, we do!" Here's why…

The longer I have served in local ministry the more I have come to realize there is a fundamental problem inherent in many churches. That problem has to do with a lack of understanding as to why we gather in the first place. Yes, all of us who attend church are able to quickly, and accurately, respond that the reason we gather is to worship God. The problem, however, has nothing to do with the reason (to worship God) but, rather, with the definitions we use, and decisions we make, when talking about the concept of "a worship service."

For me, it all begins with a deeply grounded, unquestioning belief and ownership of how life works with God as the Creator and Sustainer of all we have ever, or will ever, know. That sounds so obvious for any Christian reading this book, right? But I have been surprised many times by how often this fundamental belief seems to be lost on so many followers of Christ.

Many of us say the right words, but when it comes to practicing what those words infer, we sometimes forget our beliefs and simply act out of our own human desires and agendas.

Before you accuse me of trying to cause feelings of guilt, I have to tell you that I do the exact same thing far more often than I'd like! I am so easily prone to using my own experience, brains and agenda to "further the Kingdom," sometimes totally forgetting there is an Almighty God just waiting for me to seek HIS ideas, HIS answers, and HIS wisdom.

That's because I am a human being who is fallible.

And, after about 40 years of serving in churches as a music & worship or creative director, I have come to the conclusion that we tend to remain more eager to please those in our church first, and God second. I don't make that statement lightly. I say this based on general observation and first-hand experience.

So, when it comes to our worship of God in the gathered assembly, I feel called to boldly and, hopefully, lovingly encourage us to re-evaluate our "worship agendas."

And that is the reason I have written this book.

So, if you're ready, let's dig in and see if we can discover the difference between feeding the flesh vs. feeding the Spirit. I pray the Lord opens the eyes of your heart (Ephesians 1:18) as we enjoy this journey together.

CHAPTER 1 – TWO WOLVES

Perhaps you know this short parable…

A grandfather is talking with his grandson and he says,

"There are two wolves inside of us which are always at war with each other. One of them is a good wolf which represents things like kindness, bravery and love. The other is a bad wolf, which represents things like greed, hatred and fear."

The grandson stops and thinks about it for a second then he looks up at his grandfather and says, "Grandfather, which one wins?"

The grandfather replies simply, "The one you feed."

As I write this book, I am in the midst of (once again) trying to refocus and redirect my life towards a more physically healthy lifestyle. It has been a life-long battle that has seen victories and defeat along the way. The primary problem for me has been an over-indulgence of unhealthy foods and a very limited intake of healthy foods. (Notice that I did not say "right or wrong" foods).

The truth is that recent doctor visits have confirmed what I already knew: that my body is aging and my lack of attention to the care and maintenance of my body has finally caught up with me in such a way that I must now take measures to change things.

It is no longer a matter of "one day" addressing the issues. That "one day" has arrived!

The funny thing is, this sudden need to change actually snuck up on me very slowly and I did not even notice. But as I close in on the big 6-0, I realize that if I want to see the big 7-0 (or 8-0, or 9-0… etc.) I need to make somewhat drastic changes right now, today, this minute! The good news is, there is still time! The bottom line question for me is this: *Do I care enough about my future to actually make those changes today?*

It all comes down to a choice.

Now, if that sounded like a speech at a self-help class, I apologize. It has more to do with the same level of urgency I feel for we in the church who lead worship (from the pastors to the musicians) as well as those who attend the worship service. And it raises the same question: ***Do we care enough about the future of worship to actually make necessary changes today?***

As the subtitle of this book indicates, it is my belief that worship in many churches is far more linked to an event (a performance) rather than an encounter (His presence).

Perhaps we can ask it this way:

What is it we are FEEDING? Or, rather, WHO is it we are feeding? In our worship, are we feeding the flesh (event) or are we feeding the Spirit (encounter)? And how do we recognize the difference between the two?

Thinking back on that passage we read earlier, we can make a few simple assertions:

Feeding the flesh is built upon, and leads to, any or all of the following:

"…sexual immorality, impurity and debauchery; idolatry and

witchcraft; hatred, discord, jealousy, fits of rage, selfish ambition, dissensions, factions and envy; drunkenness, orgies, and the like..."

Likewise, **feeding the Spirit** is built upon, and leads to, any or all of these attributes: "...love, joy, peace, forbearance, kindness, goodness, faithfulness, **23** gentleness and self-control..."

Flesh-Fed Worship, then, is characterized primarily by the following: envy, factions, dissensions, selfish ambition, discord, jealousy, fits of rage and, yes, even idolatry. (We will talk about all of these later.) The other "flesh attributes" do not seem to pop up very often as related to worship but they can, and most likely have, in some congregations.

Bottom line: Flesh-Fed Worship is **focused on pleasing man.**

In contrast, **Spirit-Fed Worship** is characterized primarily by love, joy, peace, patience, kindness, goodness, faithfulness, gentleness and self-control.

Bottom line: Spirit-Fed Worship is **focused on pleasing God.**

Feeding the spirit centers around pursuing intimacy with God. As we said earlier, it is a choice that we make to delve deeper in our relationship with God, through Jesus, in the power of the Holy Spirit. It is like a craving or a desire. It is a passion. It is a purpose. It is a pursuit.

In order to fully examine the differences between the two, we need to unpack the particulars of each. As we move into this next discussion I realize that it might seem simplistic or general to the reader. It may be simplistic, but that does not take away from the truth of what we will be discussing. I highly encourage you to consider this next section with an open heart and mind –

see if God might be trying to gently massage you to shift your thinking. Here we go…

WHAT DOES FLESH-FED WORSHIP LOOK LIKE?

The crazy thing is that flesh-fed worship is sometimes difficult to detect because it so closely resembles what we in the modern age call (or have redefined as) "worship."

Most of today's churches are following (or desiring to follow) a trend and most are doing, basically, the same thing at the worship gatherings. They gather in a large room that is usually darker in color with lights aimed at the front (or stage) area. There is usually a band who leads the singing. Often times there are stage lights or soft haze or even lasers to create an atmosphere of awe. In many churches, the band is quite good, well-rehearsed, some would say "excellent" (and we will talk about that later). In fact, sometimes it is difficult to hear the difference between the music of the church praise band and the recorded version of the same songs heard on popular Christian music radio stations. On the surface, the whole package looks and sounds very good!

And the majority of those in the congregation enjoy what they see and hear.

Until…

A slide doesn't flip at the right moment…

A singer misses a word…

The vocalist is suddenly pitchy…

The drummer is too loud…

The guitar player doesn't play the guitar lick like the radio version…

One of the stage lights is flickering…

The fog machine operator forgets his cue…

In other words – everything is fine until there is a technical or human hiccup during the performance – er, uh – I mean "worship set." (#sarcasm.)

I told you earlier this book was not going to be a slam on contemporary worship. So, to help affirm that point, let me tell you that the very same scenario listed above occurs in churches who primarily offer more traditional music and worship formats. Everything in the service is fine…

Until…

A choir member falls asleep…

The organist plays too fast…

The choir director announces the wrong hymn…

The offering prayer is longer than usual…

The guest trumpet player is outside smoking…

The preacher went six minutes longer than usual…

What I am desperately hoping you see is that the issue I am speaking about has **nothing to do with so-called, "worship style."** The issue actually has everything to do with the heart of the individual worshiper.

It has everything to do – with you – and me!

So many believers are quick to criticize entertainers for being narcissistic and only doing what they do for personal glory and fame. And, the truth is, most of them are motivated by a need for attention. That is why they have chosen a career where narcissism is at the epicenter.

When I'm not leading worship, I enjoy performing as a clean comedian and while I love making people laugh, I also love the attention it brings me in that forum. No point in pretending that the only reason I tell jokes on a stage is for the joy it brings the masses. Hopefully it does help the audience to laugh and deal with the various pains of life they all endure. But, performing comedy also feeds that part of me that enjoys the attention and, to be honest, I am completely accepting of that. Why? Because of the FORUM. A comedy club is not a worship center. We are not gathered to focus on God. People come desiring to be entertained by comedy. The forum is created for entertainment – not the worship of God.

I think our top-level musical and other artistic entertainers deserve the attention they receive for their efforts to entertain us. To pretend they don't enjoy the limelight would be silly. Of course they enjoy it!

We live in the most entertainment-driven age of all time. We are long past the days of "television" being our sole source of entertainment. Now we have quality entertainment at the click of a mouse or smart phone button. The competition is huge! Just think of how many pop up ads you receive for music videos or newest songs from musicians and bands. It's really impossible to get away from the constant flow of highly produced entertainment unless you get off the grid completely – which nobody would (or could) do.

Ready for a shock? It's no different with our Christian music.

Now, this will begin to hurt a little but I won't apologize because perhaps it needs to hurt a bit in order to make a point.

There are very few differences between today's modern Christian music and secular music. On one hand, I think that is great! It reminds me of how Jesus spoke to the people of his day in simple language (parables) so that he could connect to them and they could relate to him. I do like the relational aspect of creating art that speaks to the masses in order to help them connect with God.

But on closer inspection, I wonder if we are not doing a disservice to those who attend our worship services? I wonder if those in attendance actually, and honestly, are connecting with or encountering the transforming presence of the Almighty God?

In secular entertainment there is a constant drawing of attention on those doing the performing. And the audience is encouraged to participate with passion. The act hums along with peaks and valleys until an amazing climax that can either be roaring with excitement or deeply moving.

The end result is appreciation shown by the applause, hoots and hollers of those in attendance.

Dare I say that the phrase "secular entertainment" in the above paragraph could have easily been replaced with the words, "modern worship services" and we would see absolutely nothing different in those statements. (Just for fun, go back and do that – replace those words and see how there is no difference.)

Perhaps part of the problem is that we have grown into a people, collectively, who actually believe it's up to us to "help God" by creating worship-themed "experiences" or "events" that WE believe (through research and study) will "attract" outsiders to our church and eventually lead to conversion. But please notice what I said there – "worship-themed" experiences and events as opposed to "worship" encounters.

Our culture has been a bad teacher and we have chosen to follow that bad teaching and create something that looks like worship (faux worship) as opposed to offering ACTUAL worship.

WHAT HAPPENED?

Somewhere along the line, and I'm not sure when, our worship gatherings became more about presentation than presence. This is not a new phenomenon. As a pre-teen I remember attending churches where the music was top-notch, well-rehearsed, excellently performed and unenthusiastically appreciated by those in the congregation. (We didn't call them "the audience" back then.)

It was not unusual for post-service comments to include statements like, "The music was so good today! Can't wait to hear what you do next week!" or "the choir was really magnificent today" or "that organist is amazing" or "the preacher really gave a good sermon today that I know some people in this church needed to hear!"

Both the presentation and the responses were based on feeding the flesh!

That high level of performance from the platform produced an expectation from the congregation for "bigger and better" presentations week after week.

And some of the comments were more critical:

> "Two weeks ago you sang my favorite hymn. Why don't you sing that every week?"

> "Thanks for asking me to join the choir but I'm not as good as the singers you already have."

"I noticed when you sang the anthem, the sopranos were a little off." "Took the 3rd hymn a little fast today, huh?"

Another way to view the above comments… envy, dissention, jealousy, discord, even potential fits of rage. Sounds like that list of "flesh acts" from our opening passage, doesn't it?

I need to make something very clear at this point. I am NOT saying that the music styles of days gone by did not help encourage those in attendance to worship God. I am simply saying that the manner in which that music was presented and packaged gave way to a **spectator mind-set** partnered with **a desire to ensure audience approval** – pleasing man – feeding the flesh.

One way we see this actualized in our modern worship gatherings is by the way we categorize worship. Believe it or not, when we use terms like "traditional, contemporary, blended" (or other) titles for worship service "styles" – we are focusing on feeding the flesh (pleasing man). We are not feeding the spirit when we focus on STYLES. Period.

I believe that, for a very short time (perhaps three decades or so), our church music moved away from a type of entertainment-driven, self-glorifying, flesh-fed experience. I know that, for my generation at least, things began to change with the arrival of the Jesus Movement, where church music, for the most part, while looking and sounding similar to the rock music of the day, did not stop there. It was not as simple as "creating a new type of church music influenced by rock." There was a deeper connection taking place with most of the songs during that era. People who sang were actually contributing to the worship encounter and allowing themselves to be touched and moved and changed by the transforming power of the Holy Spirit as they sang. Before that era, in many churches, sadly, this was not the norm.

Some traditionalists scoffed at this, labeling it "just emotional" (as if emotion is not part of God's creativity within each of us?) Or they found a way to diminish its importance by calling it "camp music" or similar derogatory descriptions.

Rather than scoff at the emotion I, and others, chose to embrace this new type of church music and engaging worship. (I say "new" but, really, that type of worship is quite old. A simple reading through the book of Psalms will reveal that truth.) Suddenly, believers were coming to the worship service for more than well-rehearsed, high quality "Christian-themed" entertainment. They were coming to **encounter God through Jesus Christ in the power of the Holy Spirit.**

Something was happening that transcended the "God Show" as I call it. Here is how I personally began to notice the change…

I grew up playing the piano by ear. God blessed me with a highly skilled musical ability. I also had parents who were musicians and entertainers so I was always around music and entertainment.

As I grew older my musical skills developed and soon I was playing piano, guitar, bass, French horn, and clarinet, as well as writing and arranging songs.

My church recognized my abilities to sing and play piano which led to me being cast in church youth musicals of the period as well as leading worship or providing "special music" for our worship services on occasion.

Initially, the comments following a service were, "You sure know how to play that piano, Dan!" or "Great job with the music today!" or "I wish I could play piano the way you do!" Wonderful comments of appreciation that I loved hearing.

Then, one day, God reminded me that the gift He gave me was for the ultimate purpose of glorifying HIM; of worshiping HIM. It happened in the blink of an eye, but God clearly said to me, in the middle of leading worship, "Psssst, Dan – it's not about you – it's about ME…" It wasn't mean. It wasn't angry. It was just simple, tender and honest.

And it turned worship upside down for me.

From that point on I approached playing piano, singing and leading worship in a completely different way. In my heart I knew a change had taken place. But it wasn't until post-service comments changed that I realized a true transformation had taken place.

Comments shifted. People were now saying, "I really felt God's presence today during the music" or "I was so blessed by your piano playing today" or "that song you sang really touched my heart." Do you see the difference? The comments were no longer about SKILL, they were about SOUL. The comments were no longer feeding the flesh. *They were feeding the Spirit!*

I found myself drawn to worship gatherings where the music style was secondary to the presence of God bathed in the power of the Holy Spirit. People actually drew closer to God during those times. They moved from an outside ring to an inner ring, if I can use that analogy. They chose to allow themselves to "fall into" a closer, intimate encounter with God. It made no difference what song was being sung, what year that song was written, how many instruments were playing, how many singers were singing, if someone was off-pitch, etc. None of that was what drew me closer to, or further away from, God's presence. It could have been a rock band with blasting amps or a guy alone at a piano. The thing that mattered; the thing that made the difference – was the welcoming of God's presence in the power of the Holy Spirit. And people were moved. People were altered. People were changed. As they fed the Spirit, they were fed *by* the Spirit – and it was simply beautiful.

And my assertion and observation is that this type of worship encounter is rare these days.

The problem, as I see it, is that, in recent times, our churches have reverted back to a performance-based mindset and moved almost completely away from that connective encounter with the Spirit of God in worship.

THEN...

WHAT DOES SPIRIT-FED WORSHIP LOOK LIKE?

We will discuss this further in the next chapter, but for now let me just say that if flesh-fed worship can be characterized by things like envy, anger, jealousy, fits of rage, and the like, then Spirit-fed worship must be the opposite: love, joy, peace, patience, etc.

In the end, it's all about which wolf we choose to feed.

CHAPTER 2 – FEEDING TIME

In this chapter we will take a closer look at the tension between Feeding the Flesh and Feeding the Spirit in our worship.

Let me begin by stating that I do believe all true worship is ultimately "led by" the Holy Spirit. In other words, we who lead musical worship in our churches spend time in prayer offering focused attention to the selection of songs and other elements to help our congregation worship God during the gathering.

Unfortunately, in today's mega-entertainment-driven worship culture, there is an ever-growing trend – even passion and push – to make sure we create something amazing in our services that is on par with what one might find in a stage production. Did the Holy Spirit "lead" us to that reality? Perhaps. Then again, perhaps not.

FLESH-FED WORSHIP

As I've stated earlier, flesh-fed worship is a presentation that, in theory is God-focused but, in reality, is usually man-focused. It primarily focuses on the HOW of worship, rather than the WHO of worship. In other words – it FEEDS the FLESH.

Flesh-fed worship drives us to always be striving to *please the people* in our gathering. We ask questions like, "what songs will make these people happy today?" Or, "what are the most popular worship songs on the radio right now?" It's not necessarily wrong to search for songs that will be embraced by the congregation but when that becomes the primary focus of your song selection, you are creating a "Flesh-Fed" Worship experience. (A side note is that most of today's Christian songs are designed to be performed and almost always are written in keys that are difficult for most in the congregation to sing.)

Another unfortunate by-produce of flesh-fed worship is the encouragement of criticism from most in the congregation. When the focus is on the HOW of worship (rather than the WHO of worship) we are constantly nit-picking about ways the production can be improved, often comparing it to professional worship celebrities we see in concert, or to what we hear on the radio when their songs are played. NEWSFLASH – your worship band will never sound exactly like what you hear on the radio and, if that is your goal, save time and energy and just pop in an mp3 or YouTube video of your favorite praise band and be done with it.

An obvious example of this is to simply take one popular worship song as heard on the radio. Just listen to it over and over. Really be precise about pulling out what you hear. How many electric guitars are playing? How many keyboards? Are there strings? How many vocalists? What key is the song in? How about the percussion? After you list all of those different instruments and singers, compare that to your current church worship band. If you don't have the exact same players and singers then your band will never be able to replicate what is heard on the radio. If that is your goal, you have already started at a place of failure. And if you try really hard to replicate what's on the radio (for reasons I honestly cannot fathom) then you are opening up the floodgate for criticism because keen ears in the congregation will know that your acoustic guitar opening is not that cool oboe that's heard on the recording. And they will let you know it!

Is your worship is feeding the flesh?

As Contemporary Christian music has become far more professionalized over the past few decades, we have seen an unbelievable increase in this high level of criticism among many worshipers in the pews and on the platform. It is really quite sad because it has nothing (read that again – NOTHING) to do with worship.

How do you know if you and/or your church are leaning more towards flesh-fed worship? The clues are pretty easy to spot:

People are critical of the song selection.

People are critical of particular voices or instruments.

People are critical of song styles or dates when songs were composed.

People are critical of how the band stands on the platform.

People are critical of the pastor's sermon.

People are critical of… *(do you notice a pattern?)*

Some of these critical voices try to hide behind a type of "ministry helper" mindset – as if they have been appointed by the leadership, or pastor or, dare I say it, God himself – *to fix the problems that the worship leadership must be oblivious to.*

These critical voices have actually arrived at the conclusion that the worship in the church – is "wrong" – and they have the answers as to how to fix this problem.

Let me offer a bold statement:

Worship is NEVER "wrong" – when it is truly and honestly worship. It cannot be "wrong" when it is *actually the worship of Almighty God.*

When "worship" is *really* worship, then:

The mediocre vocalist is correct (God is pleased!)

The teen playing the keyboard is correct.

The slide tech missing a few slides is correct.

The song being sung is correct.

Worship is NEVER wrong – when it is truly and honestly worship.

Yes, yes, yes, yes – I hear some of you yelling at the page. "But, Dan, we don't want distractions in our worship services!" And I agree. We don't want anything to distract from our worship of God. And the obvious culprits are missed slides, pitchy singers and poorly tuned guitars. But the other distractions are things like your heart attitude, your lack of desire to worship, your critical spirit, etc. If you are going to point fingers of "distracting blame" make sure you include yourself in that rant. Otherwise you are simply whining and ignoring the true distraction(s) to authentic worship.

In a church where I served a consultant was brought in by leadership to offer ways to improve our worship service. Between services, this consultant pulled me aside and told me to "… get rid of that girl on the tambourine…" She was not keeping the beat of the song to his liking and, in his words, she was "…ruining worship." Wow, that's a lot of power that praise team member had!

She was, apparently, able to dismantle the working and moving of God during worship because her tambourine beat was a little off here and there. I told him I was keeping her on the platform for the next service.

He didn't like that – we had meetings…

And, in the end, she remained a valuable member of our praise team.

Flesh-fed worship can be devastating on many levels because it focuses on pleasing MAN rather than on pleasing God and, in the process, it chips away at the heart and passion of those who truly desire to lead in worship.

So, let's discuss what Spirit-Fed Worship looks like in contrast.

SPIRIT-FED WORSHIP

If Flesh-Fed worship feeds the flesh, then how might we define "Spirit-Fed Worship?" (I know, the answer is obvious. Fine. They why don't more churches do it? But I digress…)

Spirit-Fed Worship focuses on the WHO of worship, rather than the HOW of worship. This is not an either/or situation – just a declaration of where the priority lies in our worship. Is it primarily focused on HOW we worship, or on WHO we worship?

In Spirit-Fed worship there is practically no room for criticism because the focus has shifted from focusing on what's wrong, to only focusing on what is right. (I don't mean what is right with the production – remember, that's flesh-feeding. I mean, what is CORRECT with the worship – in other words the focus is PRIMARILY on the WHO of Worship – the Almighty God.)

In Spirit-Fed Worship, the worshiper, the worship leaders, the pastor, all in the assembly, are SEEKING to ENCOUNTER God in the power of the Holy Spirit rather than satisfy their personal or liturgical agendas.

Spirit-Fed worship is almost never concerned about the song styles, traditions or trends, the way the band or singers stand, the year the songs were written or anything else that flesh-fed worship tends to focus on.

Spirit-Fed worship – FEEDS the spirit. Every song, every word, every prayer, every activity in the worship gathering has one focus – to glorify, adore, magnify, praise, delight in, and be transformed by, God. Those who arrive to the worship gathering bring with them the anticipation of encountering the presence of God – rather than experience the performance of a "God show."

They do not come simply to hear their favorite songs from the radio. They do not arrive demanding the great hymns they loved in their youth. They do not gather to point out how the female singer is a little "pitchy." They are not concerned that the choir is not smiling enough. Those who come to a spirit-fed gathering come to worship God.

How do you know if your church leans more towards a spirit-fed worship encounter?

People are NOT critical of the song selection.

People are NOT critical of particular voices or instruments.

People are NOT critical of song styles or dates of composition.

People are NOT critical of how the band stands on the stage.

People are NOT critical of the pastor's sermons.

People are NOT critical of… *(do you notice a pattern?)*

Since it is driven by criticism, Flesh-Fed Worship, sadly, is a major springboard to angst, turmoil and division in churches. We saw some of that described in our passage from Galatians.

In the book of James, the 4th chapter, we get further glimpses as to why this is the case…

> *"What causes fights and quarrels among you? Don't they come from your desires that battle within you? You desire but do not have, so you kill. You covet but you cannot get what you want, so you quarrel and fight. You do not have because you do not ask God." (James 4:1-2)*

Flesh-Fed Worship tends to be aligned with a "world view," rather than a "worship view":

> *"You adulterous people, don't you know that friendship with the world means enmity against God? Therefore, anyone who chooses to be a friend of the world becomes an enemy of God." (James 4:3)*

James encourages us to seek "Spirit-Fed Worship" when he writes:

> *"Submit yourselves, then, to God. Resist the devil, and he will flee from you. Come near to God and he will come near to you." (James 4:7-8)*

Really? "Resist the devil?" Sounds harsh, right? But think about it. If our worship is feeding the flesh, rather than feeding the spirit, then who is it we are listening to? (Hint: not God!)

And finally, regarding the way flesh-fed worship develops a critical spirit within those in the congregation, listen to this:

> *"Brothers and sisters, do not slander one another. Anyone who speaks against a brother or sister or judges them speaks against the law and judges it. When you judge the law, you are not keeping it, but sitting in judgment on it. There is only one Lawgiver and Judge, the one who is able to save and destroy. But you—who are you to judge your neighbor?" (James 4:11-12)*

Flesh-Fed worship feeds the flesh. Spirit-Fed worship feeds the Spirit. There is no other way to say this and we who attend church – whether we are in the pew or on the platform – really have only one choice of path that will please the Lord.

I encourage you to spend some time in prayer considering your own worship gathering. We worship leaders and the pastor are the ones who model the feeding. If you are one of the leaders of worship (music, prayer, preaching, etc.) then perhaps spend even more time on this topic and seek God's guidance and wisdom as to which pathway – Spirit-Fed or Flesh-Fed – is best for you and your church.

I think you know the answer…

By the way, later in the book, I provide simple ways for you and your church to measure which way you tend to lean – towards feeding the flesh, or feeding the Spirit.

In the next chapter we will take a look at the concept of "excellence," one of the most unfortunate and poorly defined defenses that perpetuates a flesh-fed worship mentality.

CHAPTER 3 – THE MYTH OF EXCELLENCE

The topic of "excellence" simply needs to be accurately defined and discussed so as to clearly communicate the difference between feeding the flesh and feeding the Spirit in our worship gatherings.

I recently read an article in a Christian publication admonishing church worship teams to make sure they are "excellent" in what they present on the platform. Their list of what defines excellence included things like dressing to match the younger culture, being energetic on the platform, not being over the age of 40 and not being overweight. I'll let you decide who they are focused on pleasing...

Today, it is very common for church creatives (musicians, artists, actors, etc) to use the word "excellence" as a way of defending their desire to perform their craft at a high performance standard. This is related (in a distorted manner) to how the builders of the temple used the finest materials or how David played his harp "skillfully" as a means of worshiping God in a way He is worthy to be worshiped.

Sadly, this notion has been twisted over the years to feed the flesh.

We are **not** called to be "perfect performers" for God and our perfect performance does not in any way worship God in a more profound or meaningful manner simply because of the level of performance.

As technology has advanced, so has our ability and desire to produce products that are highly performance-driven. We creatives love using the latest tech gear to create music and other art that impresses those in the audience. This is a very natural aspect of being a performance artist and there is nothing wrong with a desire to perform well in your area of creative achievement.

But let me ask some very pointed questions.

First – do you actually and honestly believe that God is impressed with your ability to play difficult guitar riffs, or sing four octaves, or compose songs with strong hooks, or to have your music heard on Christian radio?

Second – how good is "good enough…" for God?

Third – do you think God is more concerned with the heart of the artist, or the art you are creating?

To follow the logic that "God is more fully worshiped by a great performance" means that any secular entertainer (solo artist, rock band, etc.) is, by definition, "worshiping God" through their amazing performance.

Over the years, as I was continually faced with this excuse (and, yes, I do believe that, in most cases, it is simply an excuse) for demanding musical perfection based on the words, "excellence" and "skill," I decided to do a word study. I will not be offering the full extent of that word study here because, frankly, you can (and should!) do the research on your own.

What I will offer is that those words in scripture have nothing to do with performance and everything to do with ability.

In other words, when the Bible tells us that "David played skillfully" it is not teaching us that David was "**performing** for God at a high standard." In fact, all that phrase actually means is that David was ABLE to play his harp. He knew how to do it. He was SKILLED (able) to play a harp. And (here's the clincher) he used his ABILITY to play the harp for only one reason — **to glorify, and magnify, and worship His God.**

Now, I don't know David (yet!) so I can't speak precisely to his heart. But, thankfully, the Bible DOES speak to his heart — very clearly. We know, from scripture, that David was a man always seeking after God's heart. (1 Samuel 13:14)

Which causes me to ask of myself and others the obviously question: do we (me) in our musical efforts FIRST seek God's heart? Or am I first seeking to play and perform well as a musician thinking that, somewhere along the way, I might also think about God in the process.

Yeah, that probably doesn't sit well and I totally understand that. However, my years of experience in working with Christian creatives is that most of the time we DO push for better performances **first** and then find ways to make our great performance fit into some type of God- honoring moment second.

Friends – it just doesn't work that way. Really. And I just have to declare that this mindset simply does not honor God because it is focused on pleasing man (yourself or others) first.

It is no secret that many of our houses of worship are not as effective as we would like. We see mild growth and minimal impact in our communities. Many churches have a core group of rock- solid members who have remained in the church for decades through thick and thin. On one hand this is truly amazing and a real blessing. Their faithfulness has laid a strong foundation for the future of their particular church. On the other hand, this has created a type of ownership, dare I say "right," they maintain in order to steer the church the way they want, to serve their wants, needs and agendas.

This is feeding the flesh.

These churches tend to make subtle demands on music styles, worship format, service times, etc. The assumption is that these occur because of God's direction. Sometimes that is true.

Sometimes, if we're honest, this is not true.

I heard about a church who had an elder board of 12 members. Those of us who have elder boards understand that discussions can get heated over certain topics or ministry ideas. Usually, majority wins and the programs move forward. In this church, however, they did things differently. They never moved forward on any ministry or program without 100% agreement after seeking God's direction and discussion among the board members. Nothing was put in place unless all the elders – every last one – was fully on board.

While this sounds counter-productive on the surface, I have to say that I really like this practice. In a very real way, as best as they could as humans, they were truly seeking to follow God's direction for their church in a very tangible way.

This is feeding the Spirit.

I want to warn you that, if we are not careful, our call for "excellence" in our music preparation and presentation can actually **get in the way** of what God is hoping to do in our assembly when, and if, that mindset is placed as a priority over seeking what God wants to do with the musical abilities with which He has gifted us. It is actually possible for a singer whom we perceive as "pitchy" to be used by God in life-transforming ways during a worship gathering simply because that singer is anointed by God to be His voice in that moment. Sometimes the heart of that "pitchy" singer is seeking intimacy with God in a more authentic manner than "the perfect singer" and God loves, desires, honors and blesses that presentation. This is NOT a call to be sloppy or unprepared. This is a call to **seek first the Kingdom of God** and all else falls into place after that. (Matthew 6:33)

Is our desire for musical excellence feeding the flesh or feeding the Spirit? I can't answer that for you and your church – but those of you in music and worship leadership must seek the honest answer to that question before proceeding on note further in your ministry.

CHAPTER 4 – WE ARE WHAT WE WORSHIP

Worship is THE CORE of who we are and, thus, is the foundation upon which rests our relationships with one another. In a sense, we are what we worship.

We always have a choice of who we are going to feed (the Spirit or the flesh) as we interact with each other. This is true of every relationship. Every word or deed within every relationship is birthed from a desire and habit of feeding the Spirit of God, or the flesh. We are always choosing between pleasing God or pleasing man in our relationships.

This is true in our friendships and family relationships. It is true in our relationships with those who are not yet followers of Christ. It is true in our relationships with those who might never follow Christ. And it is also true in our Christian and church relationships.

CONSTRUCTIVE CRITICISM

One of the quickest means of determining if you are led more towards feeding the flesh vs. feeding the Spirit with regards to how we relate to each other is to consider how you give and receive criticism. Many of us do not welcome criticism because it usually requires us to make changes in our life – and change is difficult for most people.

What usually gets under our skin, however, is not criticism in general but, rather, the type of criticism that is offered or the way it is offered. Among believers, our usual "go to" is to teach and admonish that we must all pay attention to "constructive criticism." That's a great idea in theory however most of the time our criticisms are not really constructive. Let's consider what happens in most churches…

There is a huge difference between "constructive" criticism and "destructive" criticism. In short, criticism that does not offer a solution, but only a commentary, is not "constructive." That sort of criticism is "destructive." For example, "the slides were not in sync today" is not constructive criticism since no solution to the perceived problem is being offered. This statement is actually destructive. For this to be constructive criticism the statement would need to be said as follows: "I noticed the slides were not in sync today. Perhaps I can come by and offer your slide tech some tips on how to improve?" When we offer a criticism without any sort of solution for what we are criticizing then we are being destructive (feeding the flesh) with our relationships to one another. When we offer solutions to the issue then it becomes actual constructive criticism (feeding the Spirit) and we build unity with one another.

Another example is the congregation member who steps up after the service and says, "The band was good today but you could really use a bass player" – as if it never occurred to the worship director that a bass player would be a nice addition to the praise team. Most in the congregation have no idea what it takes for music leadership to accomplish what we are tasked to accomplish – especially in a worship culture that pushes for performance-driven services. Some churches solve this problem my offering payment and that keeps the band together. Other churches are not able to do that, or choose not to do that. Bottom line, this statement, as it sits, is destructive criticism. To be constructive, that congregation member could have said, "If you're looking for a bass player, I know a guy…" or offer another similar comment.

Let me say, once again, that a great way to measure if you are feeding the flesh or feeding the Spirit in your relationships with other believers is to carefully examine how often you are critical, and if that criticism is honestly constructive or destructive. Pointing out issues or actions that irritate us or others without adding a solution is destructive criticism and feeds the flesh.

Commenting on issues and offering a possible or helpful solution to the issue is constructive Criticism and feeds the Spirit. One leads to disharmony and division. The other leads to unity and healthy relationships.

WHAT IN GOD'S NAME HAVE WE DONE?

I mentioned earlier that one of my loves in life is performing as a comedian. Simply because of my faith, I typically perform as a clean comedian. These days I am fortunate to have opportunities to perform for churches, corporate events, cruise ships and similar venues that not only desire, but demand, "clean" comedy. The story was different when I was starting out in comedy clubs. In some ways, my "clean" sets stood out from the others as being refreshing. But many times, I was simply seen as a "goody two-shoes" and not as "funny" as the comedians who felt the freedom to toss around vulgarity like it was glitter at a bling party. My point here is not to slam "dirty" comedy.

Believe it or not, I don't really have a problem with most of that – as long as it is actually crafted well, humorous and not blasphemous towards my Lord.

But something interesting occurred as I entered the world of "club comedy." Certainly I was not naïve to the reality of two worlds: the Christian worldview – and the non-Christian world view. So, I was never surprised or shocked by what I heard or saw in the comedy clubs. I was, however, quite sad. I was sad that there were humans who were desperate to be loved and accepted and found some relief on a stage pouring out their angst through jokes. And I was also sad that, as they came to know me as a Christian, shared stories with me of how they had been deeply hurt in their lives by people who professed to be followers of Jesus.

Now, some of this was simply an excuse and I realize that. But for some, they had very valid reasons for their anger towards Christians; towards you and me.

I had to begin honestly examining how I treated other people, especially those "outside the kingdom." Do you see how even putting it that way raises a wall of division between "us" and "them?" After nearly four decades of living inside the "church bubble", for the first time in my life, I was coming face to face with the reality of how Jesus related to those around him. Was I approaching others with a mindset focused on feeding the flesh or feeding the Spirit? Was I approaching others with a sense of envy, strife, resentment, division, etc. or with a heart of love, joy, peace, patience... you know the list.

Now, it's quite easy to look at a group of "worldly comedians" (I say that a bit tongue-in-cheek) and view them as "less than acceptable" due to their lack of faith in Jesus. We Christians are so easily prone to that sort of mindset. It is a type of "Christian arrogance" we sometimes display (which might one day be the topic of a future book.) For now, just accept the fact that sometimes we do tend to view those who don't know Jesus as "less worthy" or "less acceptable" and then we subtly (or not so much!) treat them in an unworthy or unloving manner.

But you know what I found out as I interacted with those comedians? Just like me, they had issues. Just like me, they needed to be loved and accepted. Just like me, they were seeking to be understood. Just like me, they needed Jesus.

It wasn't easy for me to face those realities because I had been a Christian since the age of 12! I knew what the Bible said. I had written songs about it! I had been a worship leader! I even preached a few times! And yet, I had to ask myself honestly if, in my relationships with those "unbelievers," was I seeking to please the Spirit or seeking to please man?

While it's easy to view the obvious flaws of "outsiders" it is far more difficult to examine our relationships inside the church and determine whom we are feeding (Spirit or flesh) in those relationships.

There is a hidden, unspoken expectancy among believers to be honest, open and transparent with each other. Sometimes we are. Sometimes we open our hearts and mouths in, say, a small group or Bible study, and pour out our feelings. But often times this is not the case. Our tendency is to play it safe. We put on airs of satisfaction or contentment because we don't want to appear weak or wavering to our fellow believers. Unless our dissatisfaction is with someone else – or some church issue – then we DO tend to be verbal and open about how we really feel about the person or issue. (Did that sting a little?)

BOTTOM LINE

We are created to be in relationship with each other. That is
the great design by the Grand Designer. There is no way around
that. We cannot avoid that. We can pretend it doesn't matter, but
it does. Our relationships are eternal so it's best we learn how to
get along with each other now in ways that build up rather than
tear down. Each of us must carefully examine if, in our
interactions with each other, we are feeding the flesh or feeding
the Spirit.

CHAPTER 5 – SEEK YE FIRST...

Where do we obtain our general beliefs on our faith and on our worship? Are these beliefs and practices based on what man has told us or on what God has shown us? God HAS gifted men and women to help teach and discern His word for us – but – each of us are called to do our own research on His Word and draw our own conclusions based on what we read and, yes, what we experience.

A quick word to those out there who tend to "warn" or "guard" against experience, referring to it as more of a false or fake faith in God vs. a more intellectual approach. I won't dwell on this, but I would strongly encourage you to simply flip through the gospels and consider the things Jesus SAID is leaning more towards "intellectual" while the things he DID were more "experiential." In other words – it is not "either/or" – it is "plus/and." We should never discount "experience" when speaking of kingdom issues. Are there "false" experiences? Of course. But there is also "false teaching" so let's not assume that someone's experience is "not of God" simply because it does not line up with what your personal experience might be.

Let me ask you: Do you FIRST call yourself a Presbyterian, Baptist, Methodist, etc. or FIRST a follower of Jesus? How do you respond whenever you discover a part of your denominational heritage may not line up with scripture? Do you stick with your denomination out of loyalty – or are you willing to press forward – even if it means going in a different or new direction? Or do you stay and fight to help your denomination alter their views?

Most of us have a deep-seeded need to be loyal to something. A cause, a group, a sports team, a philosophy, etc. God has created us that way. He made us to be a people hungry to align ourselves with a belief system. Now, obviously, God wants each of us to be completely loyal to Him, through Christ, in the power of the Holy Spirit. As we noted so far, that is not always easy and it's not always our first "go to." We speak as if it is, we rationalize that it is, we pretend that it is, but, most of the time, our initial "seeking" is not what God truly wants. Most of the time, if we are honest, we just don't really stop and pray FIRST about a situation before acting.

Thankfully, we have a God who loves us so much that even our human schemes are tenderly fixed by His mighty hand and things work out okay. But do they work out the way that is best according to God?

For at least a few decades now, my approach to the leading of worship has been to make every attempt possible at first pleasing God (feeding the Spirit) instead of pleasing man (feeding the flesh). In those times when I have been successful at achieving that goal, I can honestly say that the church was "better off" or "blessed" in ways they would not have been had I not sought God first.

In your leadership of worship, selection of music, and servant loyalty to your pastor and other leaders, make sure you do all you can to seek first God's kingdom and you'll be amazed at how "all the rest" will be added – as needed – but the Holy Spirit!

CHAPTER 6 – SWIMMING WITH THE CURRENT

*"On matters of style, swim with the current, on
matters of principle, stand like a rock."*

Thomas Jefferson

As I said in the disclaimer for this book, there is no such thing as "Worship Style."

Sadly, however, the modern church has actually taken certain forms, methods, genres, trends and styles of MUSIC – and completely mislabeled them as "worship" creating what we now refer to as "worship styles."

We see churches offering Blended Worship Styles, Traditional Worship Styles, Contemporary Worship Styles, Hillsongs Worship Styles, Jesus Culture Worship Styles, Classic Worship Styles, and the list goes on.

This is a completely wrong view of worship.

Equating this to the above quote, I would say that "worship" is the principle and "music" is the style.

Please listen to this: Worship is NOT a "style." As we said earlier, worship is a response to God for all He is using all we are. Worship is a heart attitude. Worship is a posture. Worship is an acknowledgement of the wonder and awe of our Creator God, His Son Jesus in the power of the Holy Spirit.

There is no such thing as "worship style." There is only "music style."

We can have a worship service where the style of music is traditional. We can have a worship service where the style of music is contemporary.

We can have a worship service where the style of music is a blending of the two.

We can have a worship service where the style of music is country, hip-hop, Hispanic, hard rock, Reggae, or the like.

But there is no such thing as a "Worship Style."

One can, and usually does, encounter the presence of God in each of the above descriptions of worship services.

Why am I so adamant about making a clear distinction between music style and "worship style?" Because the moment we turn the worship of God into a "style preference" we step away from "the marvelous" and moved towards "marketing." We have turned worship into a THING; a COMMODITY to market and promote, rather than a BEING to magnify and adore.

This is the main reason we see so much confusion, anger and decline in so many churches today. As long as we view worship as a "style" you can promote, the focus is always on pleasing man – and what man WANTS OUT OF worship. As we discussed earlier, this can only lead to the church attendee eventually seeking a better "worship style" (show) down the street.

When we turn worship into a commodity, we end up worshiping that commodity. We end up worshiping the worship style rather than the Creator God Almighty.

Worship is our act, or response, from the heart, towards God and God alone. That response can occur regardless of what music style happens to be offered. In fact, when we are truly worshiping God with our total heart, soul, mind and strength, the music style is practically meaningless. The focus is on FEEDING THE SPIRIT, rather than FEEDING THE FLESH.

As you can tell, I believe whole-heartedly that this is massively important. And unless we make changes, the future of our churches runs the risk of crumbling before our eyes.

STYLISTIC ADORNMENTS

While we're on the topic of style, we need to touch on a few areas which have become practically (and unfortunately) essential to where modern worship has evolved. None of these, by the way, really have anything to do with the worship of God. They do, however, have everything to do with what we have come to believe are "mandatory" in order for worship to be relevant, edgy and irresistible. They are nothing more than adornments; bedazzled worship, if you will.

Nearly every ad for a "worship leader" on the top church staffing websites includes phrases that are related to the following adornments. That saddens me because it just shows how far we have drifted from the true heart of worship.

Let's look at some of these adornments.

OUR WORSHIP "GOES TO ELEVEN"

I grew up immersed in the rock music of the 60's and 70's. I have attended many rock concerts featuring many well-known bands. I have owned, and endlessly played, records, cassette tapes and CD's of top rock musicians, blaring the music through huge speakers or into well-padded headphones to the point where my heart was beating to the rhythms of the songs.

Many have tried to make the connection to loud, rhythmic rock music and the devil and, for a while, there was definitely some thought that this music was evil. (Of course, Larry Norman chastised those who maintained this notion with his famous song, "Why should the devil have all the good music." And, he was right!)

The culture of the 60's and 70's were bathed in rock music – some of it horrid. But that music style was something that communicated to a younger generation which is why the Jesus Movement became so popular. Suddenly, teens and young adults found themselves relating to the gospel message using a music format they could understand. They no longer had to strive to make sense of the thick language of traditional hymns. Instead, they found connecting points with groups like Love Song, Mustard Seed Faith, Second Chapter of Acts and others. Believe it or not, for the time, these were considered rock bands. Later, groups like Stryper, Petra and Undercover created even edgier music that also helped bring the gospel to audiences who were familiar with that type of sound.

In recent years, however, Christian bands and worship leaders have gone one step further and ramped up the volume in their song sets to such high decibel levels that many congregants will not even attend the music portion of the service. They simply wait until the message because they want to save their eardrums from destruction.

I know that some are laughing at me right now, calling me old or antiquated. Laugh if you want, but I want to plead with you that, perhaps, your desire to ramp up the volume to ridiculously high volume levels has nothing to do with the worship of God. God is not more pleased, or worshiped in a deeper or more powerful way when your worship music "goes to eleven." (That's a "Spinal Tap" reference for those even older than me.)

I encourage you to stop describing the worship in your church by style. This will be difficult because that concept is so engrained within modern Christians. But the sooner you begin changing how you describe the worship in your church, the sooner you will begin to see changes that will be long-lasting.

One of my great passions as a worship leader is to make sure I pay very close attention FIRST to who is sitting in the congregation (yes, I don't call them the audience) and then SECOND to my personal agendas for "doing" worship. Far too many worship leaders and church musicians today have flipped this priority. They seem focused on doing what they want FIRST, and then consider the worship needs of their congregation SECOND.

In the end, the responsibility of your worship and the music selected to help lead worship falls on the Senior Pastor, with the ultimate worship leadership (hopefully) coming from the Holy Spirit. That said, if your church happens to have a majority of congregants over the age of 55 or 60, then a weekly barrage of high-decibel music levels is, frankly, NOT ministering to them. It is actually keeping them from worshiping and eventually they may look for an exit strategy.

LIGHTS, CAMERA, ACTION!

Many churches have followed the lead of hugely popular church movements like Hillsongs or Jesus Culture. There is nothing wrong with those movements and many people have come to meet the Lord in those worship services.

But there are more crayons in the crayon box!

Adornments such as light shows, haze or fog machines, spotlights and more are fantastic for a theatrical production with the focus is on those on the stage. I can't imagine watching "Les Mis" without proper lighting and sound. But our worship gatherings are not "Les Mis" and the focus is not (or better not be) on the platform personnel.

The truth is, far too many of us have fallen into the idea of glamour and showmanship in our worship leadership. Never mind telling me that "this is the custom of the day and we have to appeal to modern young adults." Sorry to say this, but that is complete (you know what!)

There are many problems with producing a worship show (which is what occurs in many churches today). The biggest issue has to do with what we talked about earlier – the issue of criticism stemming from a desire to please man instead of God.

Just accept the fact that your amazing light show bathed in purple haze and blasting through five speaker clusters is only focused on one thing – you and/or your team of musicians. It is actually possible to be singing words about God or even have your eyes closed and hands raised but have your heart completely void of anything you could call "worship." (The truth is, you've actually experienced what I just stated. I can say that with confidence because I've experienced it, too.) Which takes me to the next adornment.

STAGE PRESENCE

Today's culture of worship has created a need — a demand, really — to develop and maintain stage presence. This is difficult to discuss because sometimes we really do fall into worship and become expressive from the heart. Far too often, however, what much of today's worship leadership resembles is more of a choreographed or performed expression that includes lots of movement or dance, forced hand-clapping, tender facial expressions for the slow songs and huge smiles and fervor for the fast songs.

Sometimes, specific attire is part of this presence. Worship leaders wear the type of clothing that fits the clothing trends of the period.

In and of itself, there is absolutely nothing wrong with this. I truly mean that. When it becomes wrong is when our focus has shifted from feeding the Spirit to feeding the flesh. We have to ask ourselves "why?"

Why are we portraying a certain look — rather than simply allowing the Holy Spirit to fall upon us and alter us?

The thing about the Holy Spirit is that he is timeless. He is free from trends. He is free from style. He is free from lights and volume and attire. The Holy Spirit desires for us to actually do away with all of those adornments and simply bathe ourselves in His presence to the point of deep transformation.

I encourage you to consider very strongly if the things with which you adorn your worship (volume, lights, attire, etc.) might actually be deterring you or others from encountering the Holy Spirit and his transformational impact on your life and lives of those over whom you are leading in worship.

In short, don't believe the lie that worship is a "style." Worship is only one thing – a response to God for all He is with everything you are. HOW we worship (what music we choose, etc.) is simply the collection of tools. Nothing more.

CHAPTER 7 –

POLICIES, PRACTICES and PROGRAMMING

In my previous book, "What in God's Name Are We Doing?" I speak at length about the need to be devoted to the pastors and leaders of our churches. Let me begin this chapter with a very short discussion on that concept because I believe the only way a church will thrive and grow, and be blessed, is if we follow a basic outline given to us in scripture. (In Chapter 9 I go into more detail on this passage, by the way.)

Acts 2:42-47 is a very well-known passage that has been preached on and written about many times over. I hope you take a moment to read that passage in the next few days. In short, here is what that passage tells us.

The early church chose to be devoted to the apostle's teaching. They loved one another tangibly and as servant. They prayed together. They shared in communion together. They worshiped with all of their heart and anticipated the Holy Spirit working in their midst. People were healed. Miracles occurred. All of this was built on the foundation of devotion to the pastor, leaders and one another. Verse 47 tells us that, because of their devotion, "the Lord added to their number those who were being saved."

Let me ask you a question. Have you ever overheard, or been in the midst of, a discussion where the senior pastor or staff or elders were being ridiculed or spoken of in a negative manner? That is NOT how you show devotion to your leaders. That is NOT loving your leaders. That is NOT following your leaders. That type of dialogue only leads to division and God will not bless your church no matter how large your screens are, what type of edgy music you present or how fantastic the preaching is.

It is absolutely essential that you settle once and for all this matter of who leads and guides your church and how willing you are to truly remain devoted to their leadership in the public forum.

Assuming you have settled this issue, let's now discuss how churches create policy, practices and programming.

The thinking is, of course, that there is a great amount of prayer, seeking Gods wisdom – and certainly church leaders to pray. But having served as an elder and staff member for several churches, it is my experience that after an opening prayer, the bulk of the meeting is nothing more than a business meeting with everyone sharing and pushing for their particular beliefs and agendas on what THEY think is best for the church body. This is feeding the flesh.

I recall when I served as an elder for a large church. Our board of elders had 24 members. I made the suggestion that as many elders as possible meet every Thursday morning at 6am to spend an hour in prayer for our church. The first Thursday, three of us attended the meeting. And that same group of three met faithfully for the next 2 years only joined occasionally by one or two others. While I wish more had joined us, God did move in powerful ways in our church and I believe it had at least something to do with our small group of 3 – 5 meeting on a regular basis to pray for our church.

Far too often, however, leadership can become more like a business meeting not really showing actual support of ministries and programs but simply creating policy based on personal agendas. Selfish agendas feed the flesh. They basically say, "It's not MY idea so I won't support it."

That is not ministry or servant leadership.

HOW WE PROGRAM OUR SERVICES

Before we can begin a discussion on how to program for our worship services, a very important question must be asked and answered. Basically, that question is this: "What is worship?" This question needs to be asked and answered by the Senior Pastor and board of elders or other leaders. Then, this answer must be clearly articulated to those who lead in worship, primarily the music or worship director and their musicians and other creative team members.

Once the definition of worship is settled and the path is set in place for how your church will lead worship, the discussion of music styles can begin.

I narrow down the bulk of our "church music" – that is, music that is specifically set aside for the purpose of encouraging the worship of God during a worship gathering – into two very general categories.

One category I call "Reminders." These songs remind us of God's attributes, activities and accomplishments. They tend to be songs in a third-person account, for example: God did this, God did that, how great God is for doing these things. These are wonderful songs that remind us of our amazing and almighty Creator of all. We sing these songs and recount the wonder of our

God as we nod in agreement while singing along or listening to the words.

Some have elected to categorize our classic or traditional hymns as "reminder" songs and, for the most part, that tends to be a fair assessment. However, many of today's modern worship songs also fit this category as they are third-person accounts of what God has done. They are musical testimonies, in other words.

The second category I call "Responders." These songs are far more personal in their lyric content and attitude. These songs are more of a first-person response to God using words and phrases like: You are amazing, You are a great God, I praise You, God, for who You are, etc.

Every song style we currently know and utilize in our worship gatherings includes songs written from both categories. There are "responder" and "reminder" hymns, choral anthems, children's songs, contemporary Christian songs, etc. This further helps to show that the style of a song should never be how we judge its inclusion or elimination from our worship gatherings.

Believers can choose to worship God whether a song is reminding them of His greatness, or directly responding to Him for His greatness.

The question to ask ourselves is what type of worship gathering are we hoping to see occur in our churches? Do want people to primarily reflect and remember, or do we want them to react and respond to God's presence in the power of the Holy Spirit? Or, do we want a mix of both to occur?

There are churches – huge churches – from both general approaches. I think it's fair to say that the majority of seeker-driven churches, in general, tend to utilize songs that lean more towards a reminder flavor than responder. Reminder songs are easier for the masses to accept and enjoy – or allow. This is mainly because they are not very demanding of a deep commitment on the part of the worshiper. I don't mean for that to sound cruel or judgmental just honest, and I believe it is an honest assessment of most seeker-driven churches.

It's equally fair to say that most large non-denominational or charismatic churches, again, in general, tend to use responder songs. These churches crave a more demonstrative expression in their worship and this can be seen and heard in the songs they select and how those songs are sung by the congregation.

One of the great things about current Christian radio is that you can hear both responder and reminder songs if you listen throughout the day. In fact, I encourage you to spend one day just listening to the songs on your favorite Christian radio station and see if you can hear the difference between the two general styles.

For fun, I encourage you to do the same thing with secular music – from your teen era to the present. See if you can isolate songs that are responders from those that are reminders. For example, is the Beatles' hit, "I Wanna Hold Your Hand" more of a responder song or a reminder song? How about Taylor Swift's "Shake it off?" Listen to songs that have stirred you emotionally. Which category do those songs tend to fall into? How about patriotic songs? Are these more of a reminder or responder?

The reason for all of this "homework" (ha) is to get us thinking about the songs we select for inclusion in our worship gatherings. What is our purpose of singing? Is it to remind ourselves of God's greatness and goodness? (Not a bad thing!) Or is our hope for something a bit deeper or more intimate to occur?

Reminder songs can be quite powerful, usually on a grand scale, and evoke a lot of passion. This can be great for a congregation! Responder songs, on the other hands, tend draw the singer into a more intimate encounter with the Lord during the singing.

Personally, I tend to enjoy filling music sets with both types of songs. My normal plan, depending on how the music portion of the service is designed, is to open with one or two reminder songs – "this is why we are here, folks" – and then move into two or three responder songs – "this is the God we are gathered here to worship" – and then, perhaps closing with one more reminder song just to lift our hearts to celebrate the God we have just worshiped. Notice I did not once mention any particular song style. That was on purpose. A time of worship should include songs from a variety of styles – not to please the people, but to help enforce the focus being on the WHO of worship, rather than the HOW of worship.

Obviously, we who lead the music need to work in submission to our senior pastor and elders. If our leaders are instructing us to select and lead a certain type of song style, then I believe we need to honor that leadership role because the Bible promises blessings when we do! My experience has been that, over time, as a pastor and music director get to know each other and trust each other, a bit more freedom is usually granted along the way. When that happens, it's truly a blessing!

Here is a quick little exercise...

Consider the following songs and then decide for yourself if they lean more towards "responder" or "reminder." (some might be both!)

How Great Thou Art (Hymn by Carl Boberg)

There is a Redeemer (Keith Green)

Good, Good Father (Chris Tomlin)

10,000 Reasons (Matt Redman)

Mighty to Save (Hillsongs)

These Things are True of You (Tommy Walker)

Oh For A Thousand Tongues (hymn by Charles Wesley)

Amazing Grace (hymn by John Newton)

He Reigns (Newsboys)

Sing Your Praise To The Lord (Rich Mullins, Amy Grant)

Our God Reigns (Leonard E. Smith)

God is on the Move (7eventh Time Down)

Jot down some "reminder" songs that come to your mind…

Now, jot down some "responder" songs that come to your mind…

As you set out to program the music and other creative elements of your worship service, under the guidance of your senior pastor, be mindful of the types of songs and music you employ and why you utilize them. Always keep your focus on feeding the Spirit rather than feeding the flesh and you will see the fruit of that focus blossom in your gatherings.

CHAPTER 8 – LET'S GET PERSONAL

In order to begin making positive changes and move more towards feeding the Spirit rather than feeding the flesh, we have to get personal and ask some tough questions.

First, I encourage you to visualize people you know who you consider to be critical. (It's okay, this is just between you and the Lord – I'm not asking you to judge them – just consider them.)

Now – make a list, either on paper or in your head, specifying what they are critical of. Music styles? Song choices? Tech problems? Just list the things that these people are critical of or complain about.

Then – truly consider if these complaints and criticisms are feeding the flesh or feeding the Spirit.

Now make another list. This time, think of people you just sense are desiring to please God; to feed the Spirit. When you interact with them are they uplifting and encouraging? Like the first list, jot down their names. Then, next to their names, list the things these people are critical of.

I wager that your first list is longer both in terms of names and criticisms than the second. In fact, I'd be shocked if the second list was half as long as the first.

Now, the most important question to ask: which list would your name most likely appear on? Perhaps a more pointed way to ask this is: how do others perceive you?

I would like to suggest you take a short, honest, self-assessment quiz to help focus on which way you tend to lean – towards feeding the flesh or feeding the Spirit. This will have the best results if you are truly honest with yourself. Answer "yes" or "no" to each of the following questions:

1. In general, to you arrive late to church?
2. Upon arriving, do you notice things are are "wrong?"
3. Does it bother you if the slides are out of sync?
4. Do you wish the band played different songs?
5. Do you desire the band & singers to be trendy?
6. Do "pitchy" singers bother you?
7. Do you believe a stronger performance is important?
8. Do you think the pastor is out of touch with younger attendees?
9. Do you avoid interaction with some church members?

This is not an exhaustive list, of course, but, generally, the most questions you answered "yes" to above, the more you probably lean towards "feeding the flesh." This is because all of the questions above speak to the idea of pleasing man (others and/or yourself.) None of the questions above are focused on first pleasing God or feeding the Spirit.

Let's look at another set of questions. Again, be as honest as possible.

1. Do you joyfully anticipate attending church?
2. Do you choose to worship regardless of song selections?
3. Do you choose to worship regardless of music style?
4. Do you expect the Holy Spirit to be present in the assembly?
5. Are you free from distractions during the worship service?
6. Are you satisfied with what takes place during worship?
7. Do you choose to support the pastor and church leadership?
8. Do you offer constructive criticism when needed?
9. Are you excited to tell others about your church?

Again, the more of these questions you answered affirmatively, the more you probably lean towards feeding the Spirit.

These quizzes are not scientific, just a general barometer of which way you tend to lean when it comes to worship.

REFLECTIONS ON THE QUESTIONS I PROPOSED.

Regarding our arriving on time to church.

Every situation is different, of course. However, my experience has shown me that when people arrive late to church this is usually because they are not excited to attend. Perhaps they don't like the music so they only come for the sermon. Or, they are attending more out of obligation than a true desire to fellowship with other believers. This mentality tends to be "man-pleasing" (feeding the flesh) because it is putting man's needs and wants ahead of God's.

You might be thinking, "Well, if the church offered something more exciting, I would show up on time." That mindset feeds the flesh, not the Spirit. It might be possible that the "thing" that needs to change – is your attitude!

Song selections and Music styles.

Even in our modern age this continues to be a big issue in churches. Every individual has their own agendas of what they want when it comes to music and song selection. And, most of the time, every single person has a completely different set of criteria as to what should or should not be offered in the worship service.

I am just going to boldly say that this mindset is completely counter to God's desire for us when it comes to worship. Song choices and music styles have nothing to do with the worship of God. Worship is a choice. Period. We choose to worship regardless of song selections and music styles. At least that is how things are supposed to be. When we bring with us into the gathering a personal agenda of what songs or music should or should not be utilized, we are simply focusing on pleasing man (ourselves or others) and that feeds the flesh. As I've said earlier in this book, there is no such thing as "worship style" and we really need to move away from that wrongly defined view of worship.

Production issues.

Sadly, we live in an age where the worship of God in most churches has elected to replicate entertainment we see on television or at concerts. As I said before, along with advancements in technical stage production (music, lights, etc) has come the desire to achieve the same level of production in our church services. The problem is not with the production itself. The problem has to do with our strong desire to replicate entertainment and stage performances. Why is this wrong? Because the focus of entertainment and performance is always on the stage personnel which is perfect and necessary for a stage performance, but is completely contrary and dangerous when it comes to a worship setting. The focus of the worship setting must be on God, His Son, Jesus, and the Holy Spirit's influence on the gathering. When the focus is on the stage personnel we run the risk of worshiping those who lead worship, and that is idolatry.

We have to honestly ask if our focus in on the pitchy singer, the mis-flipped slide, the song selection, the lighting, etc. If that is our focus, and we are unable to free ourselves of those "distractions," then we might need to do that thing where you cut off your hand if it causes you to sin… (Matthew 5:30). In other words – if the tech is getting in the way, do LESS of it!

Supporting the leadership.

This is such a big issue and so many of us don't even realize just how important it is. Your hallway or lunch meeting conversations about the weaknesses of your pastor, staff, elders and other leaders is completely focused on feeding the flesh. The evil one continuously whispers in our ears to be critical of the leadership of the church because when things don't go our way we seek someone to blame.

I've already spoken to this earlier but let me say it again. We MUST be devoted to the leaders God has appointed and anointed to shepherd us. Even if we don't completely love the WAYS they lead, they are still the ones God has put in place and, therefore, we need to honor and support them. When you are the pastor of a church, then you can do things your way. Until then, you either support the leadership of the church, or you leave. It's that simple. (Please don't offer me your list of "what abouts" – obviously when a pastor is completely out of line with scripture we take appropriate action. But 99% of the time, your issues with your pastor do NOT stem from heresy. Get over it and move on.)

Love one another.

Our love for one another – or lack thereof – is a strong barometer of which way you tend to lean – feeding the Spirit or feeding the flesh. Really be honest with yourself in this area. If you continue to have angst with people in your church you need to address that, seek resolve and continue on in the journey. To harbor anger or resentment or hate is to feed the flesh. Remember that the fruit of the Spirit is love, joy, peace, patience, kindness, goodness, gentleness, faithfulness and self-control.

I hope this self-assessment section has helped you focus a bit more on how you tend to lean and, if you lean more towards feeding the flesh, that you are now armed and motivated to make changes necessary to shift the focus of your feeding.

Once you have finished this self-assessment, take some time to consider the same questions (or variations of them) for your church as a whole. How does your church tend to lean on these questions and issues? If you find your church tends to lean more towards feeding the flesh, what can you do to model another mindset both in attitude and realization?

CHAPTER 9 –

STEPS TO DEVELOPING SPIRIT FED WORSHIP

In my previous book, "What in God's Name are We Doing?" I speak at length about a particular passage in scripture that I believe offers us a clear means of operating as a church and that leads to God-blessed church growth.

That passage is Acts 2:42-47 and it reads thusly in "The Message" translation which I happen to like:

> *That day about three thousand took him at his word, were baptized and were signed up. They committed themselves to the teaching of the apostles, the life together, the common meal, and the prayers.*

> *Everyone around was in awe—all those wonders and signs done through the apostles! And all the believers lived in a wonderful harmony, holding everything in common. They sold whatever they owned and pooled their resources so that each person's need was met.*

> *They followed a daily discipline of worship in the Temple followed by meals at home, every meal a celebration, exuberant and joyful, as they praised God. People in general liked what they saw. Every day their number grew as God added those who were saved.*

In a nutshell, here are my takeaways from this passage about the early church which I believe are crucial to helping us become faith communities who feed the Spirit more than the flesh:

1. They were committed and devoted to their pastors and leaders.

2. They anticipated and welcomed miraculous works of God though the power of the Holy Spirit.

3. They lived in unity with one another, loving and serving each other in tangible ways as a witness to the world around them.

4. They worshiped freely, exuberantly and powerfully.

5. They gathered together for meals and shared communion and both were times of great celebration and remembrance.

Does the above describe your church? If so, praise God! If not, perhaps it's time to make some changes. Here are some questions to consider – as you answer, make sure you do so with a desire to feed the Spirit, rather than the flesh:

1. What three things would you like to see change in your church over the next three years?

2. What do you believe are the three biggest issues or problems in your church at the moment?

3. Do you want to see the worship in your church change? If so, how?

4. What will YOU personally commit to doing about these issues?

Remember that there are two ways (in general) that these changes take place.

First, you personally make decisions to refocus your feeding. You choose to move more towards feeding the Spirit in every aspect of your life: at church, in worship, at your job, with your family and friends, etc. This is a proactive choice on your past to become more of the person God has created, crafted and called you to be.

Second, your church begins to make changes that shift their focus from feeding the flesh (pleasing man) to feeding the Spirit (pleasing God). This will be far more difficult than you might imagine for a variety of reasons. Perhaps your church as been "doing church" the same way for decades and things are just too comfortable. Or, your church leaders are concerned about numbers (both attendance numbers and dollar numbers). Or, it's even possible that your church is not as eager as you might think or hope to actually make changes that would bring about more interaction with the Holy Spirit because, frankly, it can be a little uncomfortable for some - - at first! I can tell you from experience, however, that once you and your church step over that "discomfort" threshold, what waits for us on the other side is truly amazing and life- transforming!

PUTTING IT INTO PRACTICE

Every pastor and worship leader will arrive at what works best for their church, given various factors like denominational standards and personal preferences. The following is simply one way to begin programming your worship service in a way that could help the congregation view worship less as an event, and more as an encounter:

<u>OPENING SONG(S)</u>

One or two upbeat, gathering type songs that proclaim why we have come together. Using my earlier suggestion of Reminder/Responder songs, I think one or two reminder songs might work well here. This is your music leadership, under the guidance of the pastor, alerting the gathering as to why we are joining together in worship.

A SHORT WELCOME

The pastor greets and welcomes everyone. This lead directly into an invitation for the congregation to greet one another. During that introduction, your band and musicians play softly, but energetically, in the background. Just maintain that sense of worship you began with.

CONGREGATIONAL PRAISE AND WORSHIP

This is just the title I am using. You can call this segment whatever you like. I see this lasting about 15-20 minutes and utilizing any or all of the following: Reminder AND Responder songs, prayers (from the platform and congregation), short words or phrases of God's glory, might, wonder, power, love, etc, Scripture reading(s), etc. It's always wonderful to utilize lay people from the congregation in roles where they are comfortable, for example scripture readings or short prayers. Remember that this portion is NOT "a song set" where you showcase the talents of your gifted musicians. Rather, your gifted musicians use their talents and abilities to help encourage the congregation to encounter the life-changing presence of the Holy Spirit in your midst. My experience is that it takes people time to step into this sort of connection with God and that's why the combination of songs, prayers and scripture should be given at least 15 – 20 minutes of time in the service, if possible.

OFFERING SONG

If you take an offering during your service, this is a nice place to have that occur. Again, remember that any song you do here should feed the Spirit rather than feed the flesh. It can be a performed song (meaning, the congregation does not sing along) but try to move away from the notion of creating a performance. Be excellent (the heart issue we spoke of earlier) but remember that the focus of our music is on GOD, not man and never the presentation itself.

TESTIMONY

If time allows, it's great to offer a short time for testimonies from the congregation or a testimony spotlight (live, or on video) to help remind everyone of how God is working in and thru the members of your congregation.

ANNOUNCEMENTS

The issue of "where to place the announcements" is always difficult. This is because in most churches the announcement don't feel like they add to the overall worship. Perhaps it's time to change that notion and choose to treat the announcements more like a tag to the testimonies. The testimonies reveal how God is working in the lives of individuals. The announcements can reveal how God is working in the body life of the church! For example, that upcoming All- Church BBQ Potluck can be promoted as a way for the church to get together and enjoy fellowship with one another rather than a "typical picnic" if that makes sense.

MESSAGE

Now comes a message from your pastor or teacher. In the best case scenario, this message has been nurtured and supported by the other worship elements that have occurred thus far — the songs, the prayers, the readings, etc.

CLOSING

There are many ways to close a worship service. In an effort to keep us on track with moving away from an event and towards an encounter, I suggest that right after the message you enter a time of prayer (again, time allowing) where elders or other leaders come to the front and are available to pray with those who have specific emotional, spiritual or physical needs.

As I said, this is just one way to approach how you plan and program the worship service. Along the way there will be other elements added in or differences made due to special services or other circumstances. The main thing to always remember is that we are not "event planners" — we are "leaders of worship." Don't treat the worship gathering like a well-themed "God-Event." Because that will never lead to ultimate growth. As I said earlier, when we create productions, this encourages those in the congregation to go seek a "better production" down the street.

Anyone can hire great musicians and create an exciting show. But you have the opportunity to, perhaps, be the one church in town that purposefully seeks to bring people into an encounter with the Holy Spirit during worship. Focus on feeding the Spirit and you will never go wrong!

Also – one reminder about those adornments we spoke about earlier. I encourage you to free yourself from being tempted to be trendy. Even if every other church in town is using light shows, haze machines, choreographed worship leaders and pre-service countdowns, that doesn't mean you need to replicate that. Pray as pastors, staff and leaders and honestly seek first God's desire and design for how He wants you to best minister to the people who are already walking through your doors so that they can catch a wider vision and begin inviting others to the church.

Always keep your focus on feeding the Spirit rather than feeding the flesh. It really is the best way to go!

Dan McGowan

CHAPTER 10 - CONCLUSION

Conclusions of books bother me. They seem to be a somewhat mandatory or obligatory chapter to fill a few pages at the end of the book. In most cases it is just a summary of what the reader has already been digesting and, for that reason, a conclusion feels somewhat unnecessary.

So, let me conclude by simply asking a few key questions that I hope you take the time to pray over, ponder and then consider making changes if necessary.

Who are you feeding in your personal life – your interactions with those around you? The Spirit or the flesh?

Who are you feeding in your personal worship? The Spirit or the flesh?

Who is your church feeding in their planning and execution of corporate or congregational worship? The Spirit or the flesh?

Who is your church leadership (pastors, elders, staff, etc) feeding as you plan and program your worship services? The Spirit or the flesh?

I hope this book has helped expand your view of how serious the matter is of recognizing the difference between seeking after and pleasing God or pleasing man; of feeding the flesh or feeding the Spirit.

Because, in the end, only one of those wolves is going to win…

The one you feed.

Blessings,

Dan McGowan

ABOUT THE AUTHOR

Dan McGowan is a veteran music, worship and creative arts director for local churches with a strong desire to see believers come to a deeper awareness of what it means to encounter the presence of God, through Jesus Christ in the power of the Holy Spirit, rather than simply attend or experience a "worship event."

Dan is a published songwriter and music composer, a voice-over talent and on-camera actor as well as an internationally performing stand-up comedian.

Dan and his wife, Kathy, who live in Southern California, have been married for over three decades. They have three adult children and a dog named Shay.

For information on Dan's other books and creative endeavors please visit Dan's website at:
www.danmcgowan.com.

Made in the USA
San Bernardino, CA
05 April 2017